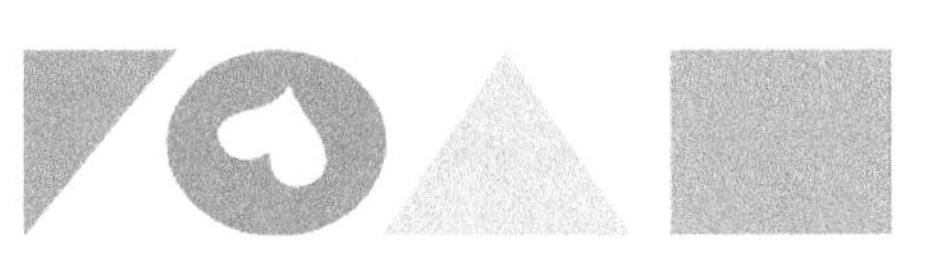

This Coloring Book Belongs To :

____

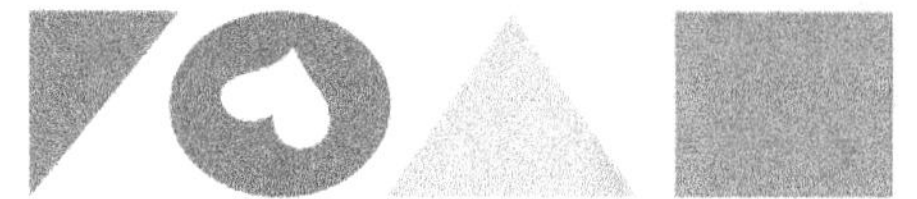

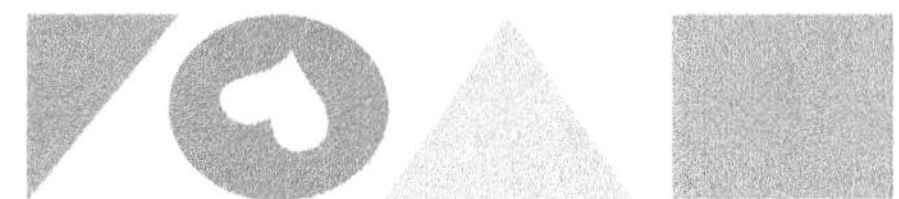

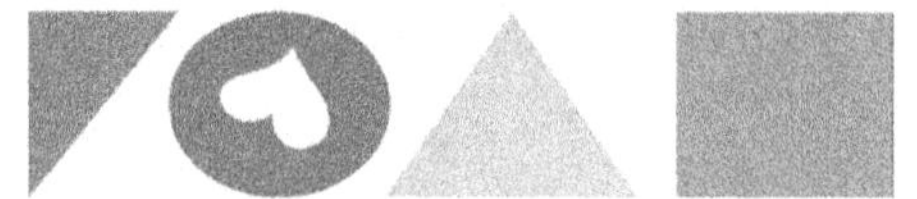

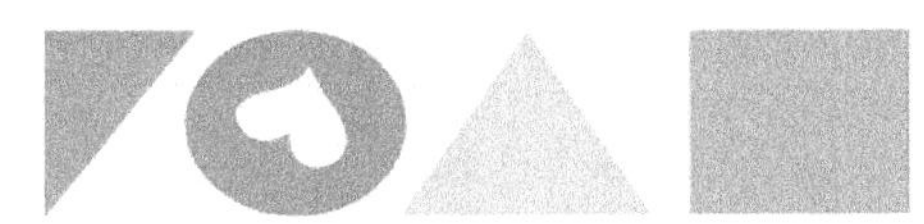

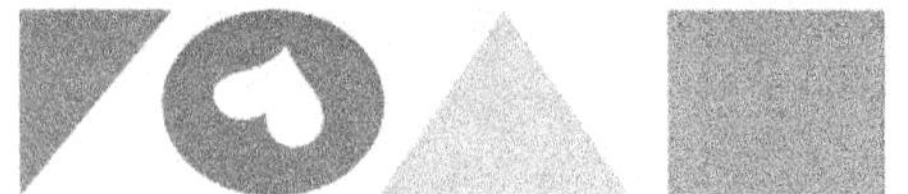

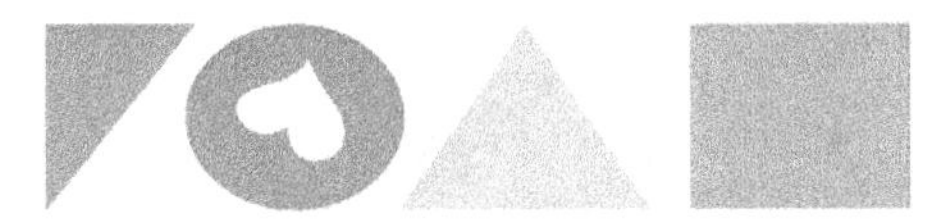

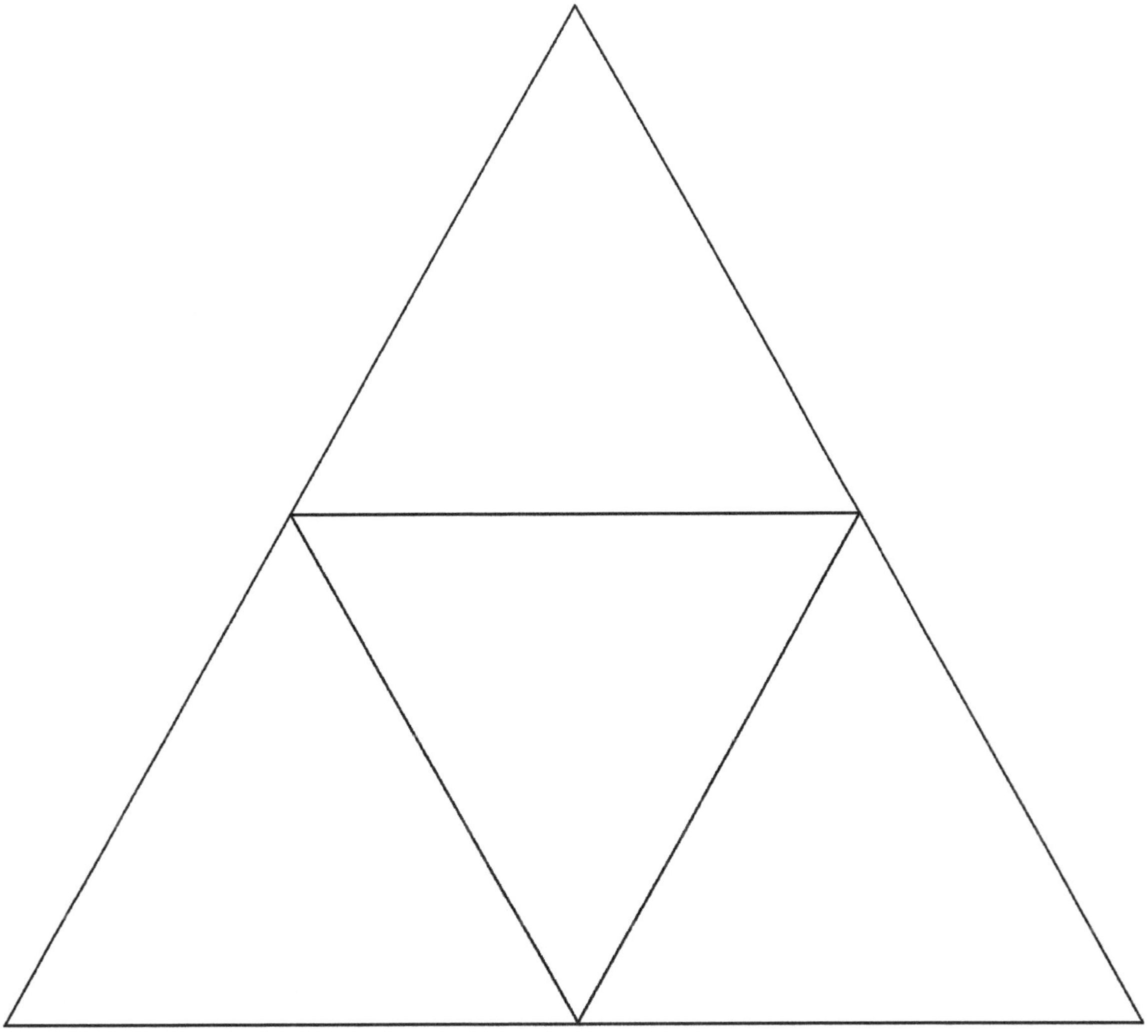

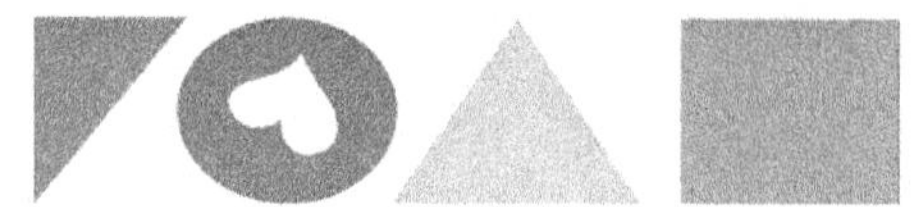

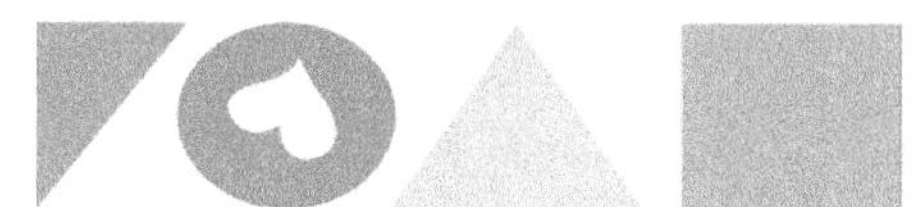

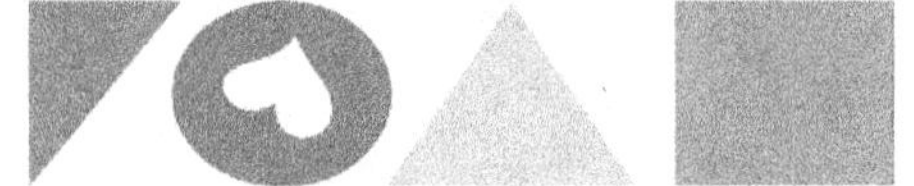

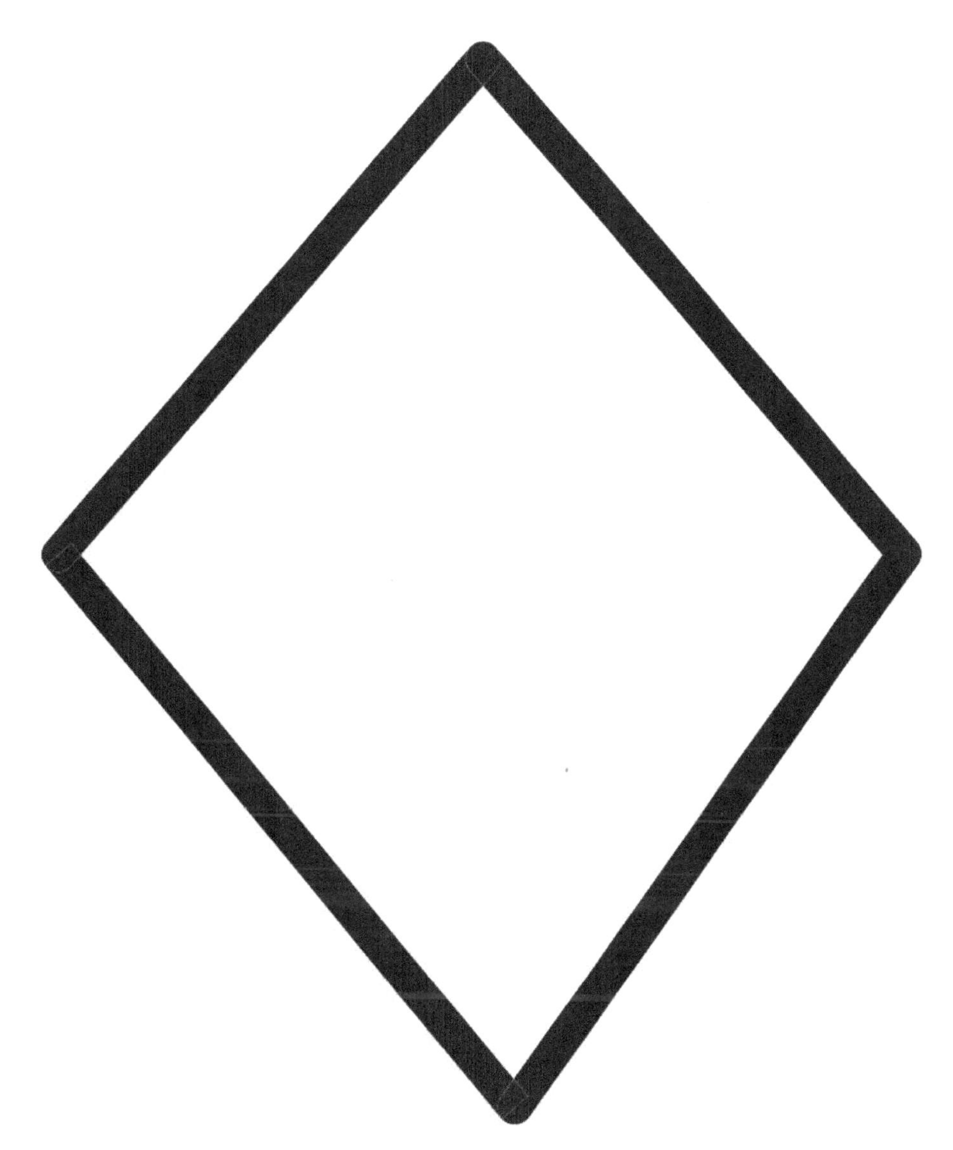

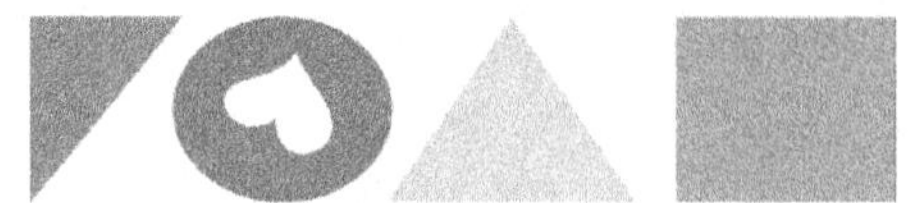

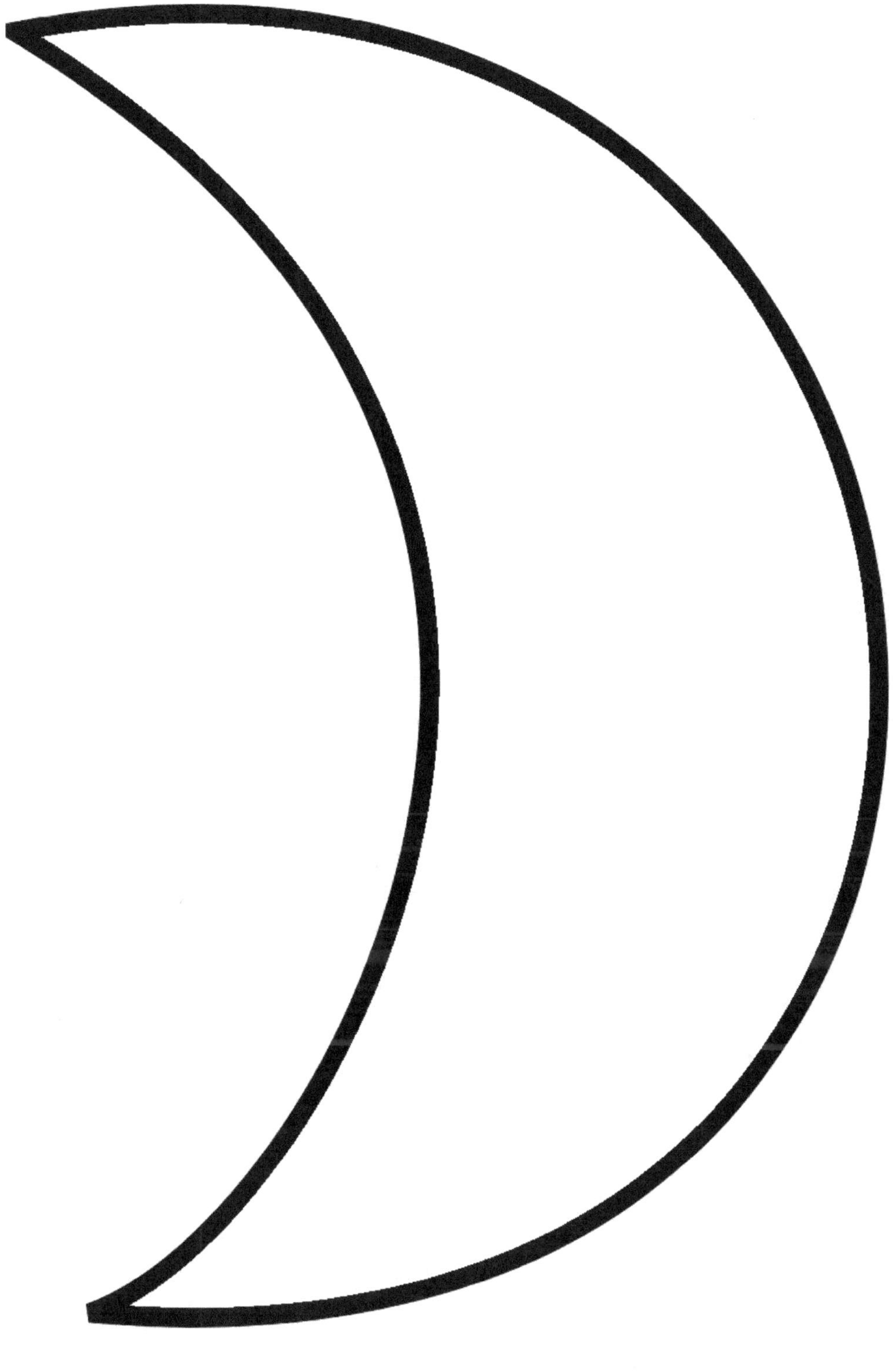

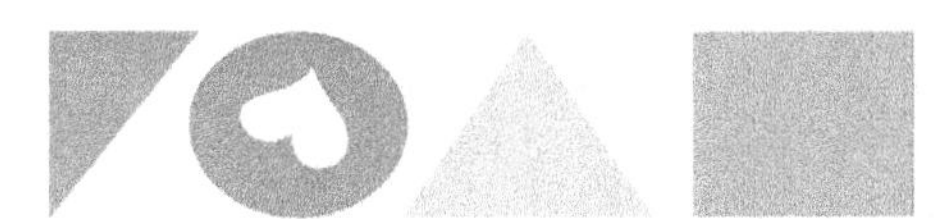

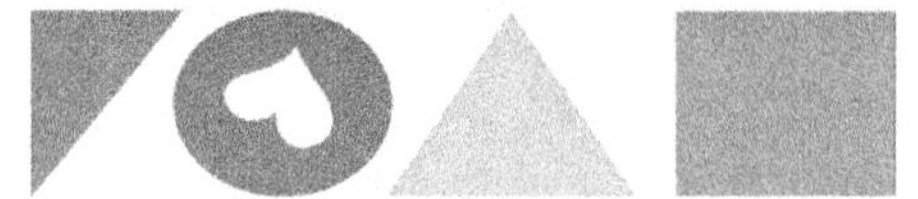

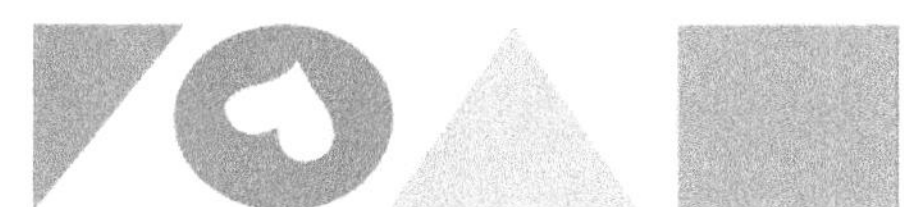
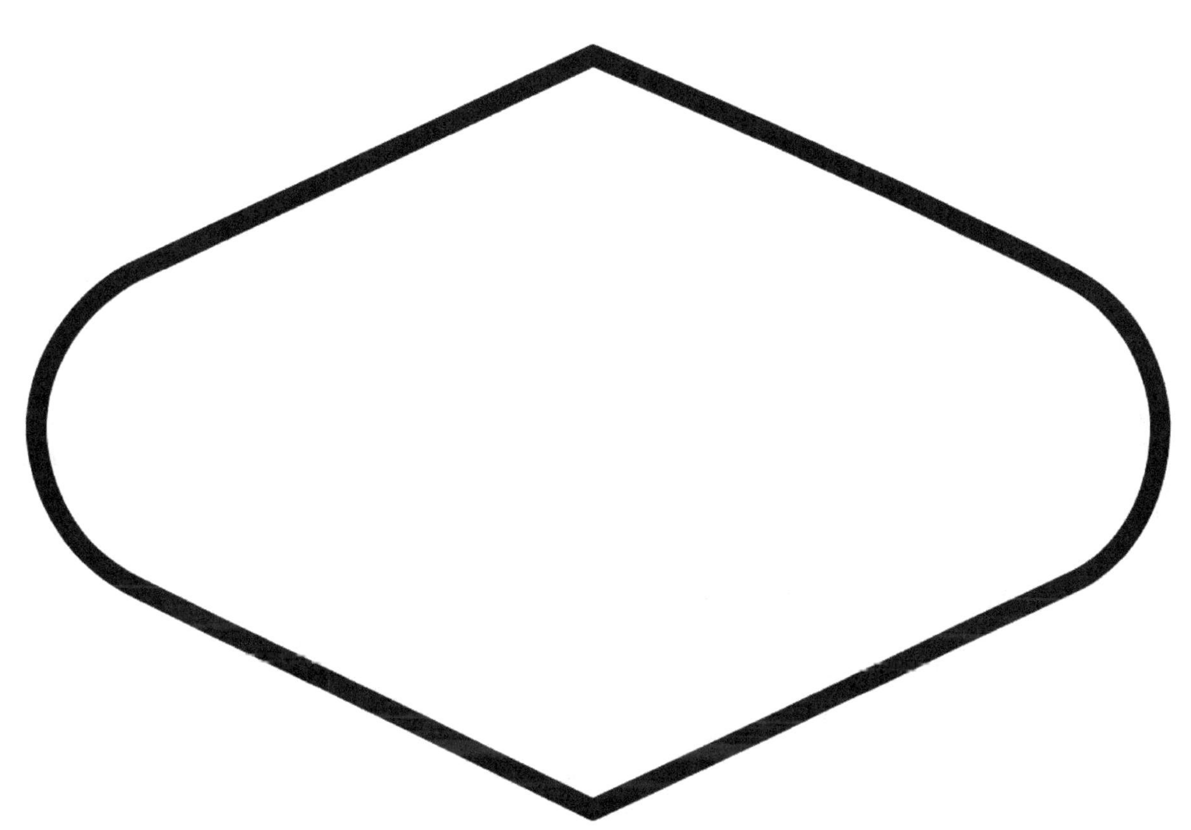

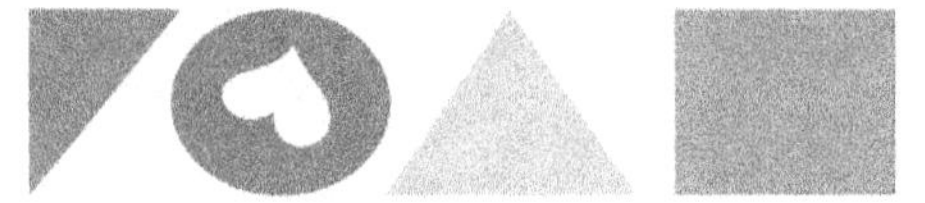

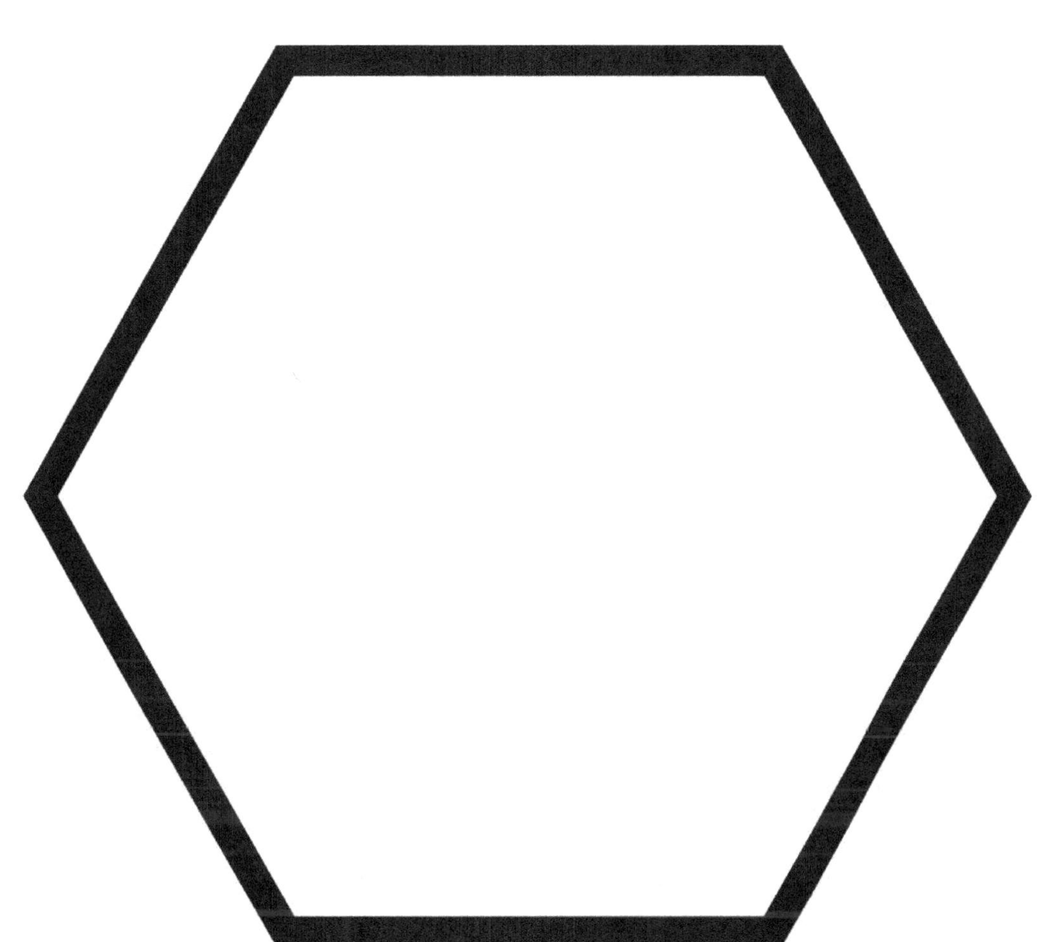

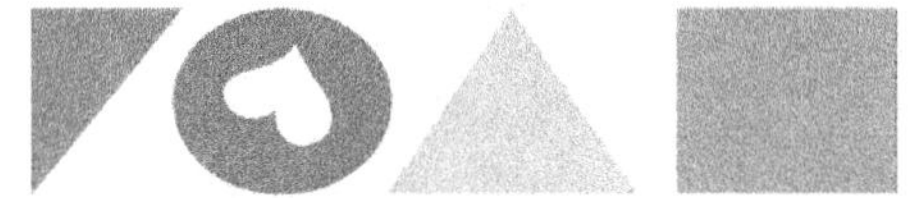

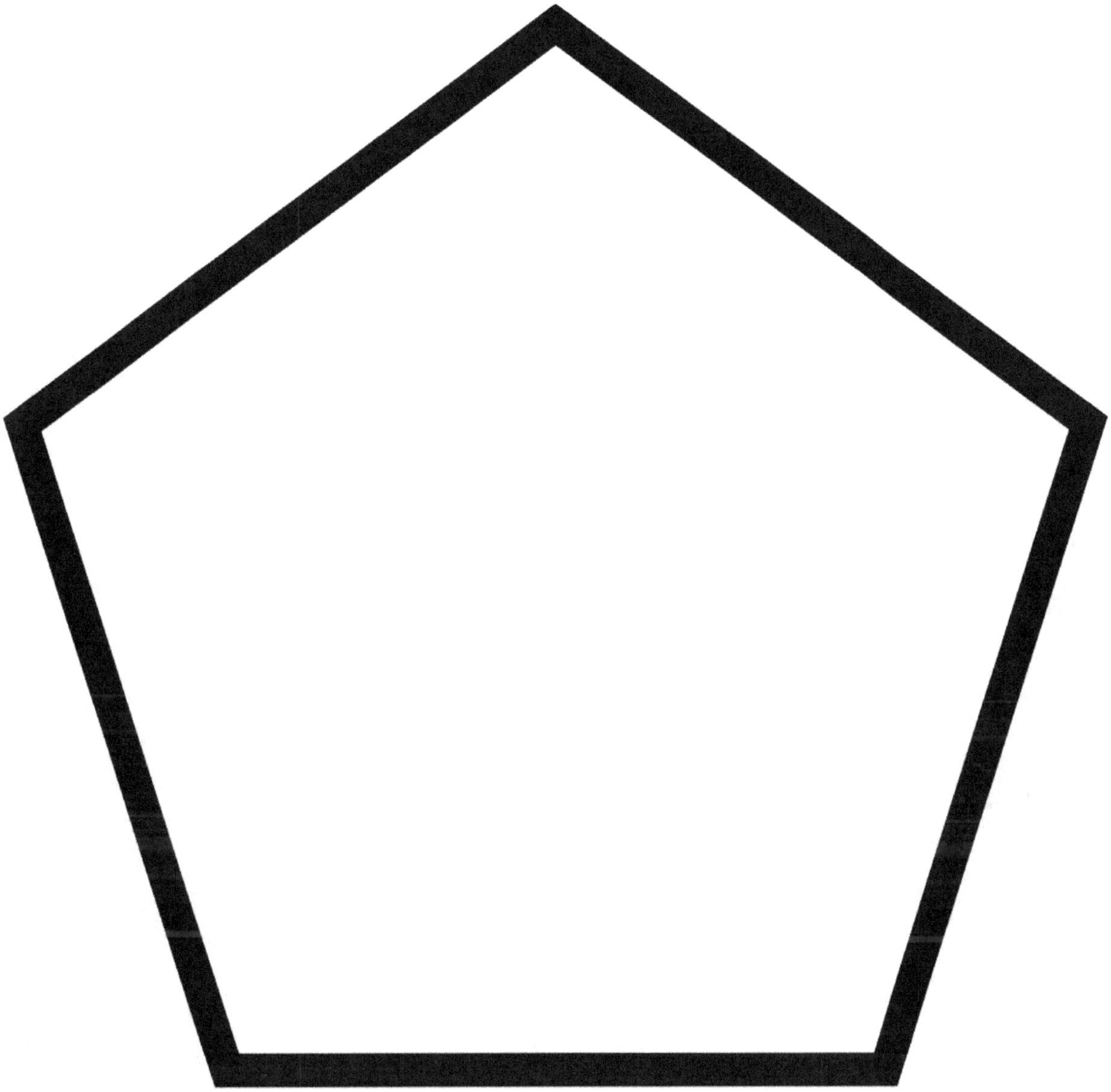

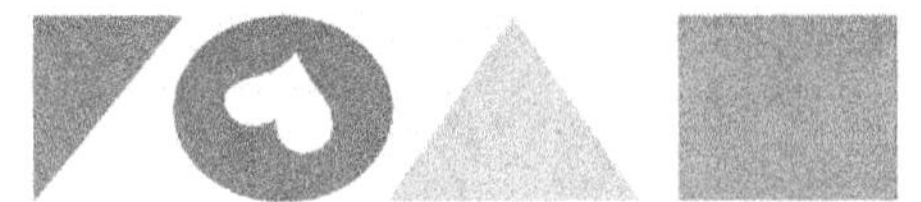

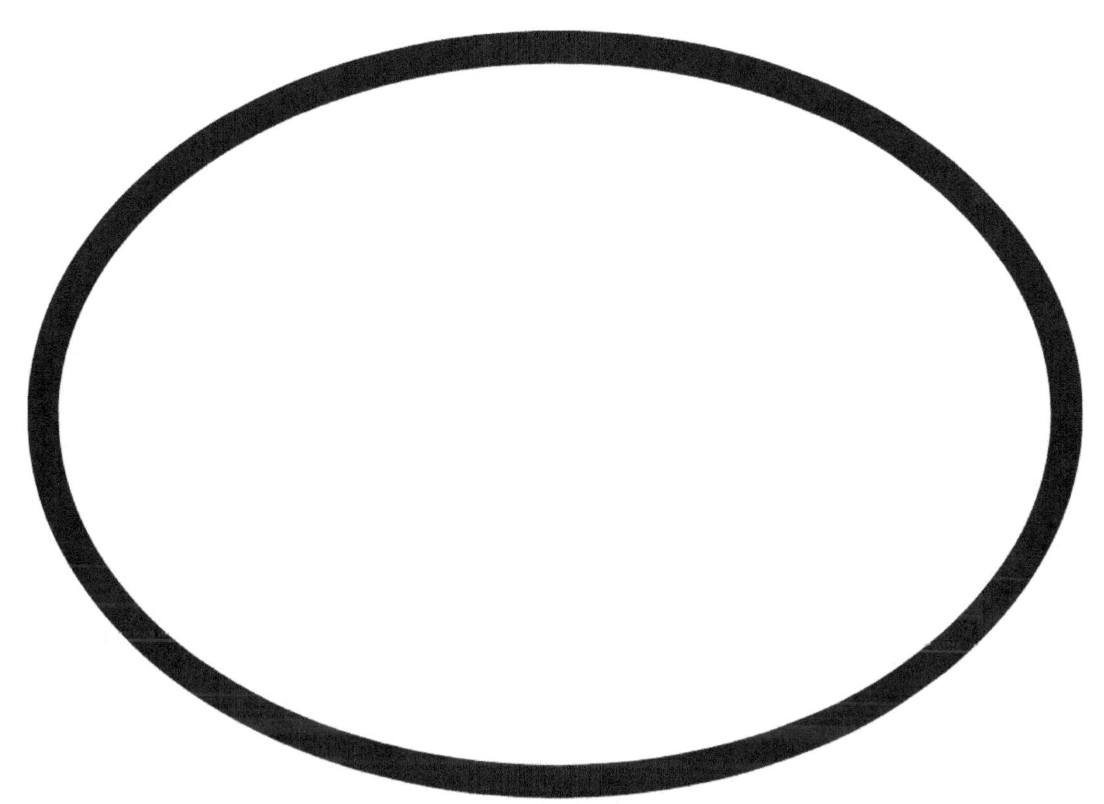

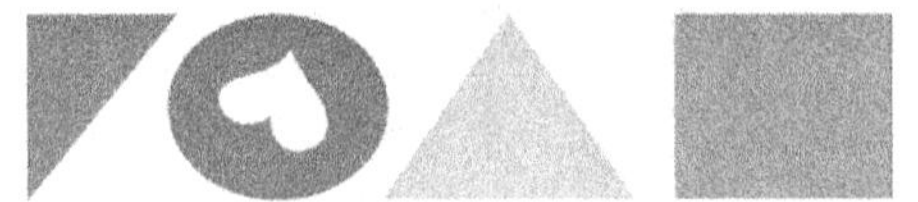

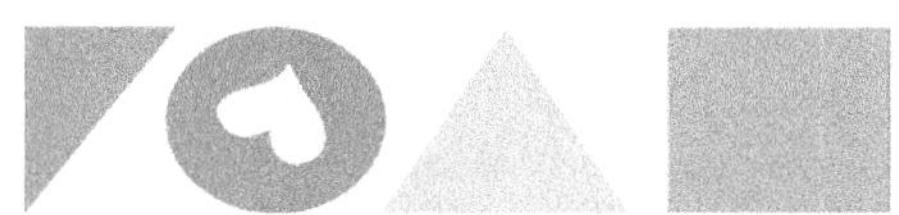

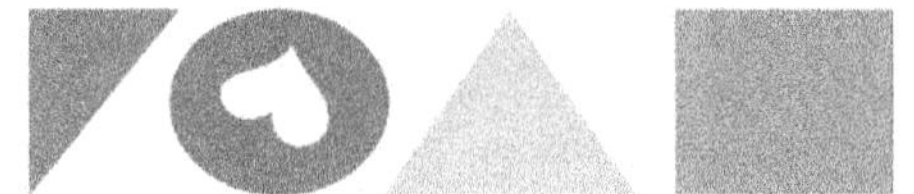

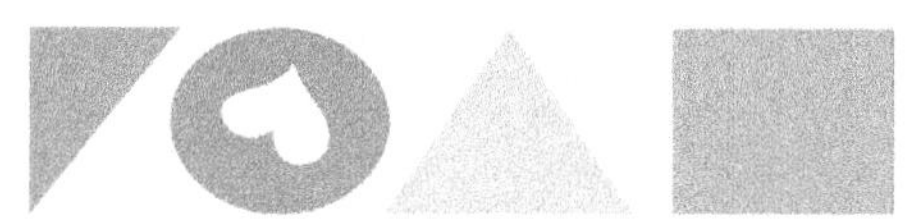

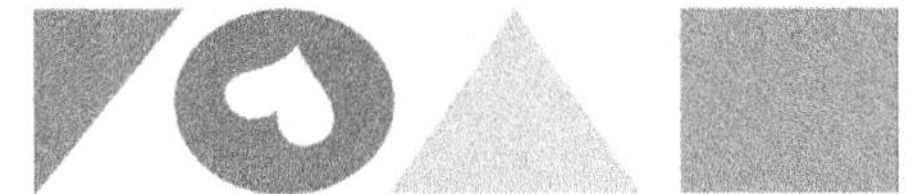

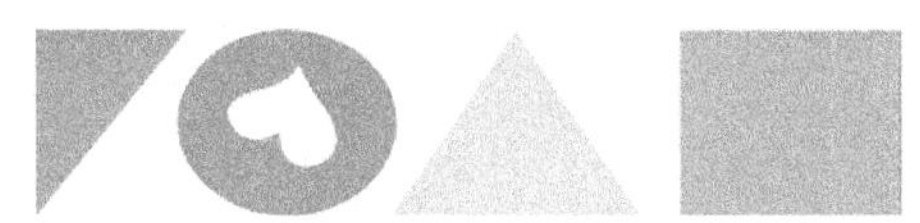

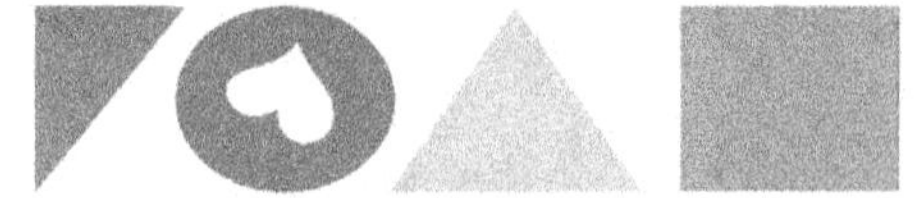